Thus Speaks Maitreya On Esa The Christ

The first edition of this book was published in August of 1991.

The second edition was published in December of 2009.

Copyright © 1991 by Maitreya

INTRODUCTION

This is a book about Esa (Jesus), The Christ. It is a collection of quotes from **Maitreya's** writings and Satsangs (Discourses) about the teacher and teachings of the Third Seal of **The Greatest Sign**.

Humanity is at a critical point in history. There are rapid changes going on in all levels of human life – socially, physically, intellectually, and spiritually. The old ways, the old systems, are no longer working, and we are moving closer and closer to real chaos and destruction (has not this been prophesied!).

The **Mission of Maitreya** is offering a viable alternative to these old systems, given by the Most High (God), through **Maitreya**, His First Begotten Son (Messiah). This alternative involves creation of the **Communities of Light** with a system to connect these communities together.

Through these communities His Kingdom will be established on earth as it is in Heaven. This is the fulfillment of the promise of the Lord that His Kingdom will come on earth as it is in heaven. The teaching of Esa The Christ is a part of the Plan which is revealed to humanity by **Maitreya**. This booklet clarifies this point. We can learn valuable lessons from his life and place in God's Plan.

OTHER WRITINGS BY **MAITREYA** WITH
FURTHER INFORMATION ABOUT ESA, THE CHRIST:

The Holiest Of The Holies (THOTH), The Last Testament

The Plan

Golden Keys Series

Satsangs (Discourses), 1991 Feast of Tabernacles

Search for more on www.maitreya.org

FOR MORE INFORMATION, PLEASE CONTACT US:

MISSION OF MAITREYA
P.O. BOX 44100
ALBUQUERQUE, NM 87124

questions@maitreya.org

TABLE OF CONTENTS

The Beginning 1

The Greatest Sign 2

The First Begotten Son Was The First Consciousness Who, By His Grace,
Reached Pure Consciousness Before Creation (Spirit of God) 3

In The Time Period Of The Last Twelve Thousand Years, The Seven Steps
Of The **Eternal Divine Path** Were Revealed To Humanity 7

The Message 11

The Symbol Of Christianity Is the Cross (✝), The Third Seal In **The Greatest Sign** 13

Esa The Christ Is The Best Example And Symbol For Humanity To Show
That The Kingdom Will Not Be Established Without Sacrifice 17

Esa Gathered Together "The People" Under His Religion, Christianity (✝) 21

With The Coming Of Christ, The Promise Of The Scepter Of Spiritual Domination
And Kingly Status (Lawgiver) Given To Judah Was Fulfilled 25

The Life 29

The Messiah Is The One Who Fulfills The Prophecies Of His Coming 31

The Name Jesus Is Not The Real Name Of The Man Who Preached The Gospels
Two Thousand Years Ago. There Is No "J" In Hebrew, And He Was A Hebrew 35

There Has Never In History Been A Messenger, Prophet,
Or Son Of God That Was Not Born From An Earthly Mother 39

The Teachings 45

The Only Thing That Christ Really Preached Was, "The Kingdom Is At Hand" 47

The Prayer That Christ Gave To Be Performed By
His Followers Taught The Kingdom Of Heaven 51

With All The Revisions That Have Been Made Of The <u>Bible</u>, A Summary Of The
Real Teaching Of Christ Can Be Found In Chapters 5, 6, And 7 of Matthew 55

Being Baptized With The Holy Ghost (Satva-Raja,
Or Fire) Is The Only True Way Of Being Baptized 61

Esa Came As A Universal Personality With A Teaching Of Equality 65

The Miracles 69

Esa Himself Did Not Want To Make People Believe In Him
Because Of His Miracles, But Because Of His Teachings 71

History Has Shown That Miracles Do Not Make Better Believers 73

The Fulfillment 79

Every Prophet Comes To Continue To Fulfill His Will. They Come Not To
Destroy Other Teachings, Or Other Prophets, Or Other Messiahs, But To
Continually Push The Will Of God To Be Fulfilled On Earth 81

The Duty Of A Prophet Or Messenger Is To Give The Message;
He Is Not Responsible If People Accept It Or Not! 85

Any Time A New Revelation Comes To Earth, Many
Are Guided And Many Others Will Go Astray 89

In The Beginning Of The Spread Of Christianity, The Followers Of Esa
Observed God's Holy Days, But After The Romans Accepted Christianity,
Their Pagan Holidays Were Christianized 93

The Return 99

As God Has Declared In The Book Of The Revelation (The Last Book In The <u>Bible</u>),
His Work Will Remain A Mystery Until The Time Of The Seventh Angel 101

The Only Sign Christ Gave For His Ultimate Return Was That
He Will Come "In The Name Of The Lord" 105

THE BEGINNING

The Greatest Sign

THE FIRST BEGOTTEN SON

WAS THE FIRST CONSCIOUSNESS WHO,

BY HIS GRACE,

REACHED PURE CONSCIOUSNESS

BEFORE CREATION (SPIRIT OF GOD).

God consists of consciousness (Father) and the creative forces (Mother). In the Beginning when the creative forces were released and the universe was out of control (chaos), God projected His Light into the universe and eventually the First Begotten Son emerged, "and there was Light" (Genesis 1:3).

***

This First Begotten Son of God is the one who proved to be worthy through his struggle, won His Grace, and overcame the power of the tama guna over his Soul.

He became God in the manifested world. He became the Messiah, who is One with The Father (Pure Consciousness) and manifests The Mother (creative forces). He is Father and Mother in flesh. That is why He is called full of knowledge (The Father) and Grace (The Mother).

He is then the prime focus for unification and the focal point of all truths. That is why He is called The Christ.

***

Any manifestation needs a nucleus. Without the atom there would be no creation or manifestation. Every atom has a nucleus. Without the Messiah there would be no evolutionary leap of human consciousness. That is why God manifested the First Begotten Son, and used Him for this important function!

***

God is in the state of Pure Consciousness or perfect awareness with control over the three gunas in the universe. Also whoever reaches this state (by His Grace) will gain complete awareness with perfect power over the three gunas of his consciousness and with whatever other power the Lord gives to him.

***

Whoever overcomes will become His son (Revelation 21:7). He becomes in His image (a son is in the image or likeness of his Father).

Such a consciousness is in Pure Consciousness, one with The Father, and the son of God (a god). He himself becomes a center and nucleus for those who recognize the truth (God) through him. He radiates the qualities of God. By his example he becomes the way and the truth, and whoever follows his way (the **Eternal Divine Path**) will reach The Father (the Truth, The Light).

However, the true radiating nucleus of the Universe and the controller of all is The Father (God), and it is He who unifies. (As **The Greatest Sign** shows, even in the state of Pure Consciousness, the unit consciousness is under the control of the Father). However, since each unit consciousness goes through different experiences, each will become unique in itself as an individual, and at the same time be a part and parcel of God (All).

In other words, God (universe) is all, and each individual is specialized through his experiences. God can manifest Himself with special qualities through each individual with different expressions. The total of the individuals (in all levels) with their qualities together manifest all the qualities of God.

***

Many have realized that God is everything and Christ is within each person. But this is not enough. In order to bring about a unified force to this higher realization, the prophesied Messiah is paramount.

So, although Christ is in each of us, a personal manifestation of the Messiah is most important. The very presence of such a being is a sign of an evolutionary leap of human consciousness.

***

The other sons of God who reached the sonhood are at the same level and One with The Father. Yet only The First Begotten Son is the Messiah! Therefore, as we can see, although John had great powers and knowledge, when the multitude came and tried to make him proclaim that he was the Messiah, he refused. He referred them to the One who will come after him, who is preferred before him (John 1:27)!

So, even though there are many who have received great commissions, the fulfillment will come when all are focused on the nucleus!

***

That brings us to realize that there is no one, no man, no Prophet or even no Messiah who is the last one. The Messiah keeps coming again and again and again, until the fulfillment of God's Plan. That makes everyone open themselves, not only to their own teachers, but to many teachers.

Being open to many teachers and the teachings covered in **The Greatest Sign** expands your consciousness. This will bring about that deeper meaning of what your own Prophet or religion has taught you.

***

IN THE TIME PERIOD

OF THE LAST TWELVE THOUSAND YEARS,

THE SEVEN STEPS OF THE ETERNAL DIVINE PATH

WERE REVEALED TO HUMANITY.

In The Revelation in the Bible, it is revealed that there will be seven churches, Seven Seals, which would be opened, and seven Angels in different periods who would bring plagues to the earth. All these seven churches, Seals, and Angels are the seven truths and mysteries which would come to the earth. Truth is always guidance to those who are ready and have overcome, and is torture to those who are attached to this external world (plagues).

***

Each of these Seals relates to one or more religions of the world, which when combined together and their significance in the history of man is understood, then it will be realized that each of the great religions of the world have only a part of the greater truth. Each one is complementary to each other as none is perfect by itself, and together they synthesize all the religions of the world and unify all under one banner (**The Greatest Sign**).

***

Only the Lamb could open these seals. The Lamb is that spirit of truth (Christ) that opened up or helped to open the truth of the seven truths (religions) to humanity, which will guide man to salvation or the state of becoming one with the ONE.

***

Also, there are seven stars. The seven stars are the seven truths that have been revealed to humanity through Christ. In addition, each star refers to the Prophet of each seal.

***

The first three of these truths were revealed to humanity before the book of The Revelation.
They are: The Far East Philosophies (Mystical Paths), which will help a person to awaken his latent spiritual forces (☯); the teachings and theme of the Old Testament, or the necessity of the establishment of the Kingdom Of Heaven On Earth (✡); and the theme of the New Testament, that not being self-centered – being humble (✝) – is necessary to establish such a Kingdom.

As it was explained, sacrifice without surrendering the result to the Lord (☾) can become a binding force in human progress toward complete freedom from all bondages. Also the sacrifice and endeavors should be directed toward the whole universe. Otherwise separation of man from man would result. So a universal point of view (✺) is necessary, or in other words, it is necessary to realize that God is everything.

After going through all of these steps, and when a person with all these realizations becomes a dynamic spiritual force (✡), he can win the Grace of the Lord and reach Pure Consciousness (卍) which is to know all, become His son, and be in His image.

***

This seven-step path has been gradually revealed, each step as one or more of the main religions of the world. The culmination of these revelations as the seventh step is revealed through the **Mission of Maitreya**, by **Maitreya** (Messiah). The **Eternal Divine Path** is the essence of the Spirit (Eternity). It is the Path to salvation, individually and collectively.

***

So, those who really have faith and love for Esa (Jesus) as their Prophet have to realize, What was his message? What was his mission when he came on earth? If they read **THOTH** and see that Esa had a special message as the Messiah to come and fulfill according to God's Will and according to the promise which was given to Abraham, then they will put him in the right perspective according to God's Will.

***

THE MESSAGE

THE SYMBOL OF CHRISTIANITY

IS THE CROSS (†),

THE THIRD SEAL IN

THE GREATEST SIGN.

If Christianity is taken as the message brought by Esa the Christ, then it is the third message to humanity, that in order to establish the Kingdom Of Heaven within and without, the utmost sacrifice (not being self-centered, being humble) is necessary.

***

It is the Third Seal (✝) in **The Greatest Sign**. It is the teaching of Christ, and the Angel is Esa. His teaching is the sharpest ("hath the sharp sword") and has a twofold meaning, literally and mystically, "with two edges."
This sword cuts through the superstitions and ignorance, dispels the darkness, and brings light and truth to humanity.

***

The sharp sword is the truth. Whoever is in Pure Consciousness will say the truth, which is sharp as a sword. The sharp sword is used only in the verses in The Revelation about the third sign, because who has the sharpest teachings among the Prophets? It is Esa. The four gospels are the most direct and sharpest teachings of the truth. They cut through the faults (if you understand them!).

***

The cross (✝), which is the symbol of Christianity, itself is representative of a balance if you add the scales on the two sides (⚖). The pair of balances is the symbol of equality.
With Christ's teachings and the understandings of his teachings, a person should come to the point where he can overcome the devil (which is the attraction to Maya and/or false ego) and be ready to sacrifice (not being self-centered) all of individual self for establishing the Kingdom of Heaven (balances). He should hunger for righteousness and try to bring equity on earth.

***

The symbolic number three which is used all thoughout the gospels and life of Christ, such as the three temptations, three falls while carrying his cross, resurrection after three days and nights, and also, being the Third Seal in **The Greatest Sign**, are symbols of being born again, to be resurrected from the lower nature (three gunas) to the higher self.
After the lower nature is overcome, one goes to the heart chakra, which is the complete unconditional Love of Christ.

***

**THE SYMBOL OF CHRISTIANITY
IS THE CROSS (✝),
THE THIRD SEAL IN
THE GREATEST SIGN.**

If Christianity is taken as the message brought by Esa the Christ, then it is the third message to humanity, that in order to establish the Kingdom Of Heaven within and without, the utmost sacrifice (not being self-centered, being humble) is necessary.

***

It is the Third Seal (✝) in **The Greatest Sign**. It is the teaching of Christ, and the Angel is Esa. His teaching is the sharpest ("hath the sharp sword") and has a twofold meaning, literally and mystically, "with two edges."

This sword cuts through the superstitions and ignorance, dispels the darkness, and brings light and truth to humanity.

***

The sharp sword is the truth. Whoever is in Pure Consciousness will say the truth, which is sharp as a sword. The sharp sword is used only in the verses in The Revelation about the third sign, because who has the sharpest teachings among the Prophets? It is Esa. The four gospels are the most direct and sharpest teachings of the truth. They cut through the faults (if you understand them!).

***

The cross (✝), which is the symbol of Christianity, itself is representative of a balance if you add the scales on the two sides (⚖). The pair of balances is the symbol of equality.

With Christ's teachings and the understandings of his teachings, a person should come to the point where he can overcome the devil (which is the attraction to Maya and/or false ego) and be ready to sacrifice (not being self-centered) all of individual self for establishing the Kingdom of Heaven (balances). He should hunger for righteousness and try to bring equity on earth.

***

The symbolic number three which is used all thoughout the gospels and life of Christ, such as the three temptations, three falls while carrying his cross, resurrection after three days and nights, and also, being the Third Seal in **The Greatest Sign**, are symbols of being born again, to be resurrected from the lower nature (three gunas) to the higher self.

After the lower nature is overcome, one goes to the heart chakra, which is the complete unconditional Love of Christ.

***

The meaning of the verse that God "would take their heart of stone and give them a new heart," has been explained in chapter two of Revelation of The Revelation in the book **THOTH**. The heart which will replace their heart of stone is referring to the Spiritual Heart, not a fleshly heart. It is the Heart in the center of the chest, which means that the fourth chakra will be opened, the place of unconditional Love (Holy Mother). It is the center of Godly Love, understanding, compassion, etc., which replaces their human love.

This greater meaning, like many other meanings of the Scriptures, has been lost. This can be realized by looking at the statues that are made of Esa (Jesus). They place a bleeding, fleshly heart in the center of His chest, a symbol of His Spiritual Heart. That Spiritual Heart is the center of understanding, which will replace the selfish heart of man, which is like a stone.

***

The things Esa did in three and a half years, the energy is still carrying on and on and on. Why? Because he was. He did not do much; he was much!

***

This third church can also refer to the third chakra.

The first three stages (chakras) make up the lower nature of man, and until they are overcome, the possibility of falling back to the lower nature and using the powers gained for selfish desires is imminent. Also the third stage is the last in overcoming the lower nature.

***

Always remember where Esa and his teachings fit into the overall Plan. He is the three, the third sign (✝). And there were three parts in Esa's mission to be fulfilled:

First, he taught and symbolically showed (by being crucified and rising again) how to overcome the lower nature (false ego) by crucifying it, and thus be born again (rise to the higher self). With this act, he replaced the unblemished lamb that was killed by those who observed Passover to receive the Grace for the next year. His crucifixion forever released the Grace, which had been taken away at the time of Adam and Eve, back to those who follow God's Laws.

Second, he came for the "lost sheep" of the House of Israel, which he gathered.

Third, he finished and fulfilled the prophecy that the scepter and lawgiving would be finished from the tribe of Judah, so consequently from the Children of Israel, and would be given to another nation.

So, he fulfilled all parts of his mission. Again we can surely realize that God never fails to fulfill His Promises and the Prophecies, which are given through His servants. They might take longer than the human expects, but they will come true eventually.

***

Therefore, Esa fulfilled a threefold mission:

    E nd the promise given to Judah,

    S acrifice (his spiritual message),

    A ssemble (gather) the people.

***

ESA THE CHRIST

IS THE BEST EXAMPLE

AND SYMBOL FOR HUMANITY

TO SHOW THAT THE KINGDOM

WILL NOT BE ESTABLISHED

WITHOUT SACRIFICE.

Christ was sent to set an example for the Children of Israel to show them how to establish the Kingdom of Heaven by sacrifice.

He came to show the Children of Israel how to establish the Will of the Lord, which is given by their sign (✡). Their sign means the Kingdom Of Heaven On Earth. He showed them that it can be done only by sacrifice (✝) (not being self-centered).

***

After Christ was sure that his disciples knew who he was, he revealed the last part of his mission, which was to be crucified and rise again after three days. The very meaning of being crucified and rising again is that whoever wants to be risen (resurrected) to his higher self has to crucify his lower self (false ego, lower nature). Only then will he be born again. This was as Christ himself taught, that one has to be born again.

The lower nature is made up of the lower propensities in the first three chakras: Excess fear for survival, temptation, excess attraction to the external world, unhealthy sexual desires, and hunger for power and prestige to satisfy the lower desires (physiological and safety). Also, in reference to staying in the earth for three days, each day can be a symbol of overcoming the lower propensities of one chakra. Furthermore, the seal (✝) is the third sign in **The Greatest Sign**, and it is the third church (Revelation chapter 2) of the seven churches.

All of these clearly indicate where Christ's teaching stands in history and why it is so celebrated by all, because going from the lower nature to the higher self is the first and most celebrated point in spiritual progress.

***

It was prophesied that when the Christ came he was going to go to the cross and be crucified. He even stalled, meaning "hesitated," for awhile and said, "God, can you take this cup from me?" Then he realized right away, "Not my will, but Thy Will be done."

***

Christ was in Pure Consciousness, which means that he was immortal. So how can you kill an immortal person? That is why they just think they killed him, but in truth he went to His Father in heaven. Indeed all Souls are immortal!

***

Sacrifice means to struggle to progress physically, mentally, and spiritually, and to help others also to progress in these spheres. It means to be other-centered, to give up "mine" and "thine" for "ours." Therefore, in the process, the false ego is crucified (✝).

***

That is the key to happiness and joy, to forget the self for a great task. It is to help others to reach higher consciousness and create an environment (✡) that allows all to reach the highest level of realization possible. So the feeling of self-centeredness is forgotten and the cause of unhappiness will vanish.

***

Sacrifice (being humble) is a must for a spiritual aspirant. However, like any other action, sacrifice can be of three kinds. It can be from ignorance, passion, or knowledge. Sacrifice that is performed for establishing the Kingdom of Heaven cannot be from ignorance. It is from knowledge.

***

Sacrificing and selflessness should start from the top of the society (the leaders). Otherwise the masses will be exploited through their sacrifices and a few will take advantage of these sacrifices for their selfish pursuances.

***

As we know, the Third Seal (the cross) (✝) is the symbol of the coming of the Christ, Esa (Jesus). Esa went to the cross for his ideal. He showed that in order to create Communities of the Children of Light, the utmost sacrifice is necessary.

Knowing the Self will be accelerated in these communities because you will have the time, support and understanding of others to be able to meditate to know God and become One with Him. Sacrifice makes such communities possible.

***

As was said, sacrifice, like everything else, can be of three kinds. It can be from ignorance, passion, or knowledge. Sacrifice for something that is not necessary and the person does not need it, is from ignorance. Sacrifice when you expect something in return is from passion. When you expect something in return, then it is really a business, isn't it? "I do something for you, you do something for me." So you are not really doing sacrifice but you are making a deal, "You do this for me, I will do that for you." Sacrifice from knowledge is when it is done without expectation, for the good of the community.

At the same time, you always have to be careful. It is just like a good plant. When you have a good plant, the soil around the plant is good. So usually the weeds start growing around it also. The weeds start trying to obtain the nutrition from the soil where the plants are growing.

Sacrificing has to be done with a very discriminating mind, so that people will not sacrifice for the weeds but for the real plants. So we have to weed out those elements that use the resources of the community but really do not give any flower, they do not give any fruit. "You know them by their fruit." If they are not giving any fruit, what do you do? They are weeds, cut them off. You have no choice. You have to say, "OK, this is a weed, now I know." Then after a while, you know all the weeds. When you see a weed you say, "Oh, that is a weed," right away.

That is why sacrificing is so important. Many communities have suffered because very few sacrificed to the utmost and many other "weeds" just ate their nutrition. Then they became thinner and thinner. Eventually they died because they did not have any nutrition themselves to continue. They just gave and gave and gave. When they no longer gave, those communities fell apart!

Everyone, even the highest person on earth, has a limit to his capacity to give. The physical body is very demanding on the energy. Therefore, you have to weed out those things that will weaken the community and only bring in those that give fruit. Then you might be able to help others to a point that they also will give fruit.

***

Even in sacrificing, there is a pitfall. After you sacrifice for a while, you might create two kinds of expectations. You might say, "Oh, I am sacrificing so much, but why is it not working?" Sometimes it feels so slow, everything is going slow and things are not happening. You put so much effort into people and things, and you think, "It is not happening." So you might become discouraged.

The other type of expectation is, you sacrifice and you do gain some results. You say, "I am such a great person. Look at me. I am the person who is doing this. Really, this Mission needs me. I am really the person running this Mission," etc. Ego comes in.

That is when the surrendering and submission (Fourth Seal) (☾) should be remembered. Surrendering means to do the Will of God but surrender the results to Him. Submission is to ideate that, "It is not really me who is doing it, it is God who is doing it through me."

With submission we become a channel for God and we do sacrifice with a discriminating mind. We weed out the weeds. We strengthen the community. Yet at the same time, we never become very egoistical. We say, "OK, God, you did a good job. Thank you very much, I will go ahead to another project, to another service for You."

***

Esa Gathered Together

"The People" Under His Religion,

Christianity (✝).

In Genesis 49:10 in the <u>Bible</u>, Jacob prophesied about the future of Judah, his tribe, and its inheritance:

*The scepter shall not depart from Judah, nor a lawgiver from between his feet,
until Shiloh come; and unto him shall the gathering of the people be.*

Here are two prophecies which should have been fulfilled through the tribe of Judah. First, the promise of spiritual kingly domination which was given to Abraham and his seed would be fulfilled through the tribe of Judah. This is the scepter, lawgiver, and the Messiah (Shiloh) who would come from this tribe. However, the scepter and lawgiver would only stay with the tribe of Judah until the Messiah came, "…shall not depart … , until Shiloh come." Second, when the Shiloh (Messiah) came, he would gather the people under his banner, "and unto him shall the gathering of the people be."

Who were the people that would be gathered unto the Messiah? They were the ten lost tribes of the House of Israel, "the lost sheep of the house of Israel," who were gathered together as Christians under the banner of Christ. Also the Kingly spiritual domination was finished from the tribe of Judah (House of Judah).

That is why Esa said that he was "not sent but unto the lost sheep of the house of Israel."

***

This sentence is the key to understanding one of the greatest prophecies and Plans of the Lord which has been hidden from humanity for so long. A clear understanding of this great point also shows the legitimacy of Esa as the Messiah, and that God exists and is guiding the creation and history.

***

Christ had come to save those who were true seekers but were lost because of the confusion of the teachings and ideas at that time. These were the ones who saw his truth, either when he was alive or after, and rejoiced in it and were saved. They were the lost sheep of Israel who should have been saved, because it was the Will of the Father that those who have struggled to progress spiritually to the Father should be saved.

***

During his ministry, Esa went to the well of Jacob in Samaria which was given to Joseph. In this land, the people believed in him. This shows the significance of the people of Samaria with the mission of Christ. They also became the means to transfer the teachings of Christ further to the rest of the House of Israel in order for the prophecies of Jacob to be fulfilled and for God to be glorified.

***

Eventually "the House of Israel" moved toward the west and northwest of Europe. Indeed, that is where Christianity flourished and gathered all the lost Children of Israel under one religion.

***

Also in the gospel of St. John we read:

> *And this spake he not of himself: but being high priest that year, he prophesied that Esa should die **for that nation** [Jews]; And not for that nation only, but that also he should **gather together in one the children of God that were scattered abroad**. (John 11:51-52)*

Esa should have been crucified "for that nation" (the House of Judah) and also to "gather together in one the children of God that were scattered abroad."

Also, he came to "gather together the people" or as it was prophesied, to "gather together in one the children of God" – not all the children of God, but "that were scattered abroad."

"And not for that nation only" but for "the children of God that were scattered abroad" from that nation (Children of Israel). Who were those that were scattered abroad and lost? They were the House of Israel. They were the ones whom God had predicted would be scattered from the seed of Jacob (Genesis 28:14). (For further explanation, read the book <u>Children of Abram (Abraham), All Prophecies Are Fulfilled</u> in **THOTH**).

It was these people who were scattered abroad that would be blessed with the unconditional promise given to Abraham when he obeyed God even to sacrifice his sons for Him. This promise will be in effect to the end of the last age.

***

With The Coming of Christ, The Promise Of the Scepter Of Spiritual Domination And Kingly Status (Lawgiver) Given To Judah Was Fulfilled.

As it was explained, the spiritual king (scepter) should come from the tribe of Judah, and he did. Not only did all the great kings of Israel come from this tribe, but also Esa The Christ, who was from the tribe of Judah, came as the expected Messiah. His spiritual message was that in order to establish the Kingdom Of Heaven On Earth (✡), sacrifice (✝) – to be humble – is necessary.

But the historical effect was his coming as prophesied by Jacob (Israel) to finish the promise of the scepter given to the tribe of Judah.

***

The right of having this privilege no longer belonged to Judah, "The scepter shall not depart from Judah, nor a lawgiver from between his feet, until Shiloh come; and unto him shall the gathering of the people be" (Genesis 49:10).

***

The promised Messiah (Shiloh) came as Esa The Christ. He fulfilled all the signs that were given for his coming, but the Jews rejected him. He came to show the way of establishing the Kingdom of Heaven within and without, but the Jews had many concepts about the new Messiah. They expected him to come and place them in a position superior to others. They expected him to be similar to the kings they knew, with material glory and power for suppressing others, because of their wrong conception of Jewish superiority.

***

With the rejection of Esa The Messiah and the fulfillment of the prophecies of his coming, God took away the prophethood from the Jews and gave it to other nations, as was prophesied by Israel (Jacob).

This event is shown in Matthew 21:43, "Therefore I say unto you, The Kingdom of God shall be taken from you, and given to a nation bringing forth the fruits thereof."

With this sentence, the great struggle of the Jews started, but they did not believe the words of the prophecy told by Christ. However, it does not matter if humans accept or reject a Prophet. Messengers of God (Angels) are only the warners and have a message for the people. What they say will happen even if their words are not accepted. Also in the case of Esa, his crucifixion was a part of his mission.

***

Therefore, the scepter and the lawgiving were removed from the tribe of Judah and given to another nation.

This other nation was the Arabs. The spiritual kingly personality was Muhammad. The spiritual truth and laws were Islam (☾) and the Koran. The spiritual message of Prophet Muhammad can be understood from the very word "Islam." Islam comes from the word "tasleim" which means to be surrendered and/or submissive to the Will of the Lord.

With this, another prophecy was fulfilled, and also history is the witness of this truth which God promised would happen. Furthermore, nothing happens without His Will. So if a person is able to establish a new great religion, it has been His Will, even if some people do not understand it or do not like it.

***

The Life

THE MESSIAH IS THE ONE

WHO FULFILLS

THE PROPHECIES

OF HIS COMING.

When the Jews found out that their customs and beliefs were so diluted that they no longer had the original foundation, the people started to long for a Messiah to guide them to the right path. That is when the coming of the Messiah was prophesied by many Prophets.

So the expectation arose, and many prophecies came to the Jews in symbolic language. They created expectations and concepts of how the Messiah should be and in what manner he would come. Even in this aspect there was not a common agreement between different groups.

***

We can see there are a lot of prophecies in the Bible about the coming of the Christ, Esa. Christians always refer to that part of the Bible for the legitimacy of Esa being the Christ, the Expected One, the one for whom they were waiting.

We also see in Genesis that when God talked with Abraham, God said, "You are going to have a son by the name of Isaac." Abraham fell in front of God and said, "Let Ishmael be blessed." He did not believe that he was really going to have another child when he was 99 years old and his wife was 90 years old. He did not really think he was going to have a child. So he was asking God, "Let Ishmael be blessed, do not worry about another child. You know I am not going to have another child. Anything you want to give to a new child, just give it to Ishmael."

And God said, "He is already blessed." God gave the blessings of the scepter and territory to Abram, before his name was changed to Abraham. After He gave these promises, Abram had a son by the name of Ishmael from Hagar. Then He changed the name of Abram to Abraham, and He changed the name of Sarai to Sarah. He promised him another son, and promised him new land for his second son Isaac.

***

God promised Abraham that He would give two gifts to his children. One was a kingly spiritual domination (scepter) and the other material property as the birthright. These two gifts as promised were inherited from Abraham to Isaac, and then to Jacob (Israel). At the time of his death, Jacob separated these inheritances and gave the scepter (kingly spiritual domination and lawgiving) to Judah. The birthright was given to Joseph and his seed.

That is why the great king of the Children of Israel, King David, is from the tribe of Judah, and also Esa, the King of the Jews (House of Judah) is from the same tribe. Abraham is the father of all the Hebrews, so he is the father of Esa also, and David is the king and from the tribe of Judah, so he is also the father of Esa. That is why Esa who became Christ is "the son of David, the son of Abraham."

However, as Christ himself said to the Pharisees in Matthew chapter 22, verses 42-45:

> *Saying, what think ye of Christ? Whose son is he? They say unto him, The son of David.*
> *He saith unto them, How then doth David in spirit call him Lord, saying,*

The Lord said unto my Lord, Sit thou on my right hand, till I make thine enemies thy footstool?
If David then call him Lord, how is he his son?

No one could answer this question. But what is the answer? The answer is that Christ, or the First Begotten Son of God who became Pure Consciousness (Christ Consciousness), was in the world even before the creation of this manifested world. So spiritually he could not be the son of any mortal man, not even David or Abraham. However, in a fleshly sense, he was born from a mother with Jewish ancestry and from the tribe of Judah. Christ also is a consciousness, and a person.

Also Esa was conceived from a virgin, so in truth his birth was a miracle and no worldly man could claim to be his father. He was in Pure Consciousness even before coming to this world. He came to the earth as an Avatar (god-man). That is why he is called Emmanuel ("God with us"). But even an Avatar does not know he is a god-man until later on in his life when he realizes himself and understands his mission.

Furthermore, Christ was incarnated as the first Adam who guided other humans to the path of the spirit (path of Pure Consciousness) and later on as Noah, and Abram (Abraham). In fact, God had promised to Abram (Abraham), "and in thee shall all families of the earth be blessed." The only way that all families of the earth could be blessed is by Abram (Abraham) being incarnated in so many different nations and situations, and bringing the truth and blessing to them. So whoever any nation or people consider as their father or the one who brought to them the blessings, is none other than Christ. God never fails in His Promises.

***

God also told Abraham that his son Ishmael was blessed. We see the children of Ishmael are whom? They are the Arabs, and they have a great territory, stretching from Arabia all the way to the end of North Africa, and it goes to the Strait of Gibraltar where the Mediterranean connects to the Atlantic Ocean.

So God promised two things to Abram and Abraham. He promised a territorial promise, and a kingship or scepter. The territory of Isaac went to the Children of Israel, and as we said, their king, who eventually manifested as the highest kingship with spiritual power, was Christ, Esa.

He gave the same promises for Ishmael. That territory is where the Arabs live, and their highest spiritual authority came from Muhammad, their Prophet.

So you see, if you go through the prophecies in the <u>Bible</u> for the coming of the Christ, you see also there are promises and prophecies for the coming of Muhammad. So God promised to both sons of Abram (Abraham) that they were going to have a territory, and they were going to have a kingly dominating spiritual force coming from them.

If the Moslems, Christians, and Jews realize that, we can see that more than half of humanity is blessed through Abram (Abraham) and his two sons. If they can become one by just realizing these prophecies from God and their fulfillment, then they can realize the rest of **The Greatest**

Sign also is from God. It explains and clarifies those things that humanity has not yet realized.

If they do realize this, what do we have? We have unity. We have converted humanity to that for which they pray. So we have conversion. They will be converted to see the whole Truth of the unification of all the religions together.

Of course, you need some expansion of the mind. You have to be prepared for it. If you are a completely dogmatic Christian, you do not want to hear about this. But that is OK. The human situation, I hope, will become better, but it is first going to become worse. Humans eventually have to reach a point to see that what we are trying to tell them is the truth, and they have no choice but to be(come) unified.

***

THE NAME JESUS IS NOT THE REAL NAME

OF THE MAN WHO PREACHED

THE GOSPELSTWO THOUSAND YEARS AGO.

THERE IS NO "J" IN HEBREW,

AND HE WAS A HEBREW.

All those who have studied the name "Jesus" and its origin agree with one thing: It is not his original name. The most common explanation is that "Jesus is the Greek form (equivalent) of the Hebrew name Y'shua." In Latin the "Y" is pronounced "J." How the rest of the name "-shua" was transformed to "-esus," there seems to be no reliable explanation on earth.

***

So, if his real name was not Jesus, what was his name? He had two names. One was his sacred name, which is the name of the Messiah (יהושוה). The Messiah always knows his sacred name. As it is not pronounceable, we put the Hebrew equivalent for it. The Jewish people never uttered the name of the Lord. If they uttered the name of the Lord, they would be stoned to death, because they knew the real name of God cannot be pronounced. So anything you call God on earth, is not His name.

It has been revealed to us that the name Jesus comes from Zeus. The "Je" ("Jay" sound) means victory, and the "seus" means the god Zeus. Have you ever heard about Zeus, the Greek god? After Christianity was accepted in the Roman Empire, the name of Esa, which was the earthly name of Christ, was changed to "Jay" (victory to) "Zeus." Jay means victory. Zeus means the god Zeus. So Jay-Zeus (Jesus) means victory to Zeus. That is how his name became Jesus.

In the East, people know Jesus as Esa, Esa the Christ. Even in the writings about Christ that they found in a monastery in India, the name had been referred to as Esa.

***

Similar sounding names also can be found in Hebrew, for example "Esau" and "Isaiah." In Arabic and many other languages, such as Persian and Hindu, he is also called "Esa." That is why whenever the name Jesus is used in our literature to identify him for the western audience, the name Esa is also included to let them know his true birth name.

Therefore, his earthly name was Esa and his sacred name, which cannot be pronounced, is written in Hebrew with the five letters יהושוה. That is why we use that as his sacred name and Esa as his earthly name. Jesus never was his name.

So that fulfills another prophecy that, "Many will come and tell me that we cast out principalities in your name. And I say, 'I know you not,' you are the workers of iniquity," because they are not really using his name (יהושוה) to cast out the devils. They are invoking the name of Zeus to cast out the devils. So that is why he told them, "No, I do not accept your work. Your work is not done in my name. You are casting out the devils not in my name, but in the name of others."

***

The Sacred Name was also known in Islam. In a story about Muhammad, someone asked him, how many names does God have? He answered, "3000. Of these, 2,999 are revealed to humanity." The One which is kept secret is His Sacred (Holy) Name.

The creative energy (the movement felt within when repeating The Holy Name or The Word silently inside) created by the words (when the Name of the Father and Son merge as One) is the Mother (The Holy Ghost).

***

In the prayer, "In the Name of the Father, the Son and The Holy Ghost," the Name of the Son is used in the middle between The Father and The Mother to show that he is the mediator to manifest them in the manifested universe.

Without the Son, the qualities of The Father and The Mother would remain un-manifested!

***

THERE HAS NEVER IN HISTORY BEEN

A MESSENGER, PROPHET,

OR SON OF GOD

THAT WAS NOT BORN

FROM AN EARTHLY MOTHER.

The expectation that He will come from the sky (heaven) is true. But sky or heaven means Pure Consciousness. He comes from Pure Consciousness. He is an Avatar.

Cloud means confusion. Whenever the earth becomes weak and confusion prevails, His Spirit will arise on earth (Bhagavad-Gita 4:7).

***

Look at every Great Prophet. Moses, Abraham, Muhammad, Christ, etc., all were born from a woman. They were raised in the society. They were apparently regular people. Suddenly they realized their mission and then the message became the most important thing in their lives.

***

After Esa's spiritual eye was opened, his true struggle in overcoming the power of the tama guna started. That is why he was led to the wilderness, which is a symbol for the turbulent, uncontrollable mind. In this wilderness of his turbulent consciousness, he started the greatest battle in his life, the battle of overcoming the lower nature which leads man to all kinds of attractions, desires, attachments, greed, or Maya. John opened his eyes, but it was Esa himself who should have to overcome.

In the Bible (Matthew chapter 3), it is after Esa overcame the temptations of evil that he again became Christ. He has to overcome in every lifetime in order for him to recognize his Christhood.

***

Never has a Savior come who has saved all instantly, and never will there be. It is the wishful thinking of the childish character that believes this. Each person has to grow – the Savior can show the way – but it is you who has to walk it.

It is like a seven year old child to say, why doesn't his father, who is the head of the university, just give him a doctorate degree without him going through all the years of training in elementary school, high school, etc.? We are here to learn many lessons. No one can be saved until he or she is ready.

***

The difference between the man Esa (Jesus) and the Christhood of Esa was that Esa was an Avatar (god-man). He was god because he had come from Pure Consciousness. He was man because he was in the body. That is why he called himself a son of God (god) and also a son of man (man).

In his Divine state he was Christ, and in his human body he was the man Esa (Jesus).

***

Because Esa was born an Avatar (from Pure Consciousness to flesh) he remembered very well that the goal of the life is to be(come) Divine, and one of the ways to reach this goal is to follow and live, "by every word that proceedeth out of the mouth of God." By following His Will, then sustenance will be provided.

A man who only lives for bread (physiological and safety needs) is bound in his first chakra and cannot emerge from being earthbound.

***

All of the things happened in Esa's life, such as the wise men coming, Herod being informed of the child so that he became fearful, and then Mary and Joseph being forced to go to Egypt, so that the prophecies "by the prophet" were fulfilled.

Also, by Esa and his family moving to Egypt, they came in touch with the Egyptian spiritual knowledge and were influenced by it.

***

Esa went to Persia, to India, and to Tibet, and he studied with all the people there. Actually if you look at the teaching of Esa, it sounds very much like Krishna's teaching in the <u>Bhagavad-Gita</u>: "I am the way and whoever comes to me will reach the Father-God." It is very, very similar. When you read the New Testament and the <u>Bhagavad-Gita</u>, you see so much similarity there. It is the same Spirit.

***

I do not believe that he really studied much. He just picked up from the Spirit. He was their revealer for many lifetimes! The doctors were saying, "This twelve year old boy knows a lot." He knew, but not of the book. I do not think anyone can learn all these things by reading only, but the Spirit of the Father comes through him and tells him the truth.

***

Esa The Christ came as the expected Messiah. He came in a humble way and preached the gospel of the Kingdom of Heaven to the Jews. But they expected him to come from the "cloud" and in the way that had been symbolically described by the Prophets. So the Jews, because of their concepts, did not accept him as the Expected One.

He also thought differently than the beliefs of the Pharisees and the scribes of the Jews. This created a barrier for the Jews to follow him. The Jews were waiting for the Messiah to come and purify their religion. When he came and tried to break those misconceptions and purify it, they started to resist him. That is always a great obstacle when any new teaching comes to humanity. **The concepts of previous religious leaders become a barrier to accepting the new teachings.**

The reasons for the differences in the teachings of the Prophets are twofold: (1) because the mission of each Prophet is to reveal a different part of **The Greatest Sign**, and (2) because the consciousness of the human has been prepared each time to accept the new Revelation. That is why Christ said, "You do not put new wine into the old skin." Also if the Messiah comes and teaches what the people already know, **then what is the need for his coming**?

***

The Teachings

THE ONLY THING THAT CHRIST REALLY PREACHED WAS, "THE KINGDOM IS AT HAND."

Christ started his mission and the first thing he told everyone was that God's Kingdom was at hand. That is why he came to earth and that is what God's Will is. That is what God's desire is, to create His Kingdom on earth. He wants to be the King. When we accept Him as the King, then everything else will fall into place.

If we concentrate on small little things, and we think that we are the doers, then things are not going to happen the way we want. How many people are trying to take care of the poor and needy? They have been trying for centuries and thousands of years. Are they gone? Are we rid of the poor?

But when the Children of Israel accepted God as their King, as their only focus, what happened? The poor were taken care of. They became prosperous. Their whole city became so full of wealth that the silver coins were like stones in the streets. Even the children were playing with the silver coins because they were not worth anything anymore. They were so prosperous that they did not need them any longer. The gold coin was the norm.

So it depends on where our focus is. Are we going to learn our lessons, ever? Even Christ said, "The poor are going to be with us forever," as long as our focus is to take care of the poor.

But if our focus is on God, and if we accept Him and create the **Communities of Light**, what will happen to the poor? They are going to be taken care of. There will be plenty of food for them. The poor will never be homeless or helpless or foodless.

We can see that Christ also does not preach to take care of the poor. He says, "The Kingdom of God is at hand." Let your focus be on God: Not that, "I am God myself," but on God, the Father, the Spirit.

***

Both John the Baptist and Esa preached the gospel of the Kingdom of Heaven. When Christ started preaching, the mission of John was finished and the work of Esa began. However, he also brought the same message and showed the way, "Repent: for the kingdom of heaven is at hand," that only with repentance and change of heart can the Kingdom of Heaven be established (within and without). This is the same message as John's. He did not say, "I will forgive you without you repenting and changing the way of your life," but "The first step was shown for you to take, 'repent.' Then after that I will help you to progress and enter the Kingdom."

***

There are three Kingdoms Of Heaven: The Kingdom Of Heaven In Heaven (✡), the Kingdom Of Heaven On Earth (✡), and the Kingdom Of Heaven Within (✡) (all three are shown in **The Greatest Sign**).

However, the three Kingdoms become as one and under the rulership of the Lord when all of humanity repents from their egoistical ways, accepts and establishes His Laws, and creates the Kingdom Of Heaven Within and On Earth (the Kingdom Of Heaven In Heaven is already established). Only then will His Kingdom come and "His Will be done on earth as it is in heaven."

That is why both John and Esa preached that the human should repent of his selfish ways if he wants to establish the Kingdom of Heaven. They did not preach, "We have come to save you." They taught that it is up to each individual to repent, turn away from selfishness, and follow God's Laws.

***

Christ came to fulfill his mission which is a part of God's Mission. So by accepting Christ, by accepting Muhammad, by accepting the Prophets of the Old Testament, by accepting the beginning of the creation, the reason God created this creation, and that He wants His Kingdom to come on earth, then we can see that we are fulfilling God's Will. We are bringing God's Will to earth.

***

We are here to strengthen all these things. We are not for one country, for one culture, or for one people, but for the whole earth.

***

A lot of preachers preach the truth but do not follow what they preach. That is why Esa said, "Listen to what the Elders say but do not do what they do." That is because the human has two parts. He has mind, or intellect, and he has heart. It is very easy to go to the library, find a lot of books, and read about Spirit and God. It gives you some knowledge that you can talk about. But to live what you have heard or read, comes from the heart.

Sometimes you can see people who live it without ever having read anything about it. They have opened their Hearts. They are very joyous. They love God but probably have never read a word about God. They can sing God. They can praise God. They can Love God. They can be in Christ Consciousness. So they have their hearts open but their minds have little knowledge of it.

However, the best one is he who opens both of them. He opens his Heart to God so that he can live It without even knowing too much about It, and he opens his mind by reading about Him, so he can share Him with others. This will bring harmony between his Heart and his mind. Then he will not only live It but be a channel for Him.

That is actually another part that we are working toward, to bring the East and the West together. The West is a symbol of the mind. It works with intellect. And the East is the symbol of the Heart. Easterners are very emotional. They love God but probably most cannot write about Him.

Now we are approaching a time when a balance between Heart and mind is possible. Now both East and West can open their Hearts and so have the Compassion and Love of God, and have a good mind so they can read and intellectually understand God on deeper levels.

***

Many gain some spiritual powers and misuse them to show their spiritual progress and impress others (use of spiritual powers can also be from three kinds: Ignorance, passion, or knowledge). Many also use a name, which is not His Sacred Name, to do these things. But they are not acceptable, "…I never knew you" (Matthew 7:22-23). In fact, spiritual power will be given to a person to test him to see if he will fail in handling it or will use it for the right purposes. These powers should be used for His Will (establishing the **KOHOE**).

***

Christ did not say we should escape the world. Christ said, "Be in the world but not of it." He did not say forsake the world and go to the mountains and forget about it. He did not say that. He said, "Be in the world but not of it."

***

The meaning of the first and second resurrections?
The answer to this question can be found in more detail in chapter 20 of <u>Revelation of The Revelation</u> in the book **THOTH**. The first resurrection is the awakening of those who will reach Pure Consciousness in the Golden Era which is fast approaching.

When the Kingdom is established on earth, there is going to be a period of tranquility, progress, and great realizations. Following this period, which is symbolized as "one thousand years," another period of confusion will appear. After this period, again many will reach Pure Consciousness. This is the second resurrection!

***

THE PRAYER THAT CHRIST GAVE

TO BE PERFORMED BY HIS FOLLOWERS

TAUGHT THE

KINGDOM OF HEAVEN.

This prayer is well known by many:

Our Father, Who art in heaven.
Hallowed be Thy Name.
Thy Kingdom come.
Thy Will be done, on earth, as it is in heaven.
Give us this day our daily bread.
And forgive us our debts, as we forgive our debtors.
And lead us not into temptation, but deliver us from evil.
For Thine is the Kingdom, and the Power, and the Glory, forever.
Amen.

This was the prayer given by Esa. Before starting to pray, the ideation of respect and devotion toward God should be invoked. That is why the first verse gives praise to the Lord, "Hallowed be thy name," the same as "We pay our salutations to the Father."

The second verse is an expression of the desire that the Will of the Lord be done, which is for His Kingdom to be established on earth, "as it is in heaven." As it was explained previously and as it is shown in **The Greatest Sign**, there are three Kingdoms Of Heaven: the Kingdom Of Heaven In Heaven, the Kingdom Of Heaven Within, and the Kingdom Of Heaven On Earth. The Kingdom Of Heaven In Heaven already has been established. When the Kingdom of Heaven Within (✡) and the Kingdom Of Heaven On Earth (✡) are also established, then His Kingdom will come and His Will, will be done on earth as it is in Heaven. So in this verse the Will (Desire) of the Lord has been expressed. He desires to see that His Kingdom come and through it the whole universe progress as rapidly as possible toward the goal (Pure Consciousness).

"Give us this day our daily bread." To do His Will and/or before starting any spiritual progress, man's physiological and safety needs should be met. That is why the daily bread (minimum necessities) should be provided for all.

"And forgive us our debts, as we forgive our debtors." We forgive those who have done wrong to us, and the Lord will forgive us also. Forgive and you will be forgiven.

"And lead us not into temptation." The essence and reason for any wrongdoing is temptation, when an action seems good to us to do, but in reality is against the Laws of the Lord. When temptation comes to the person through his lower nature, it is a great task to overcome it. Also temptation occurs because of the power of the tama guna (crudifies the consciousness) and attraction to Maya. So in truth this verse is similar to the sentence, "We open our hearts to Your Grace and pray for Your Guidance in overcoming the power of the tama guna over our Souls, and detaching ourselves from Maya," or "lead us not into temptation, but deliver us from evil (tama guna, Maya)."

"For Thine is the Kingdom, and the Power, and the Glory, forever." He has complete power over the three gunas and is the Master of the universe. So only He can deliver us from evil or the power of the tama guna and help us detach ourselves from Maya. He is the only subject of praise in the universe, and only with directing all our attention and our being to Him can we be delivered from the ocean of Maya. So "the Kingdom, and the Power, and the Glory" are His forever.

The "Amen" is the same as "Aum" or "OM" (ॐ), which is to invoke the Lord or the Divine vibration in the universe.

***

The sooner we create the Kingdom Of Heaven On Earth, the sooner we go back home. So let us get on with it.

***

With All The Revisions That

Have Been Made

Of The <u>Bible</u>,

A Summary Of The Real Teaching Of Christ

Can Be Found In

Chapters 5, 6, and 7 Of Matthew.

There are many commandments and principles that are written all throughout the earth and in the Scriptures. Although their existence is necessary and inspiring for man, as long as they have not become an integral part of a person with God's Grace, they will not have a lasting effect.

This truth was revealed to humanity around 2,000 years ago when Esa gave the "Sermon On The Mount" in chapter five of the gospel of St. Matthew in the Bible. The Children of Abram (Abraham) had the Ten Commandments since the time of Moses and even before! However, they violated them all throughout history from the very beginning.

That is why Esa taught that the goal is not, not to break the Law, but to reach a point where no desire is left to break it. The goal is not, not to commit adultery, but to reach a point where no desire is left even to look with lust upon a woman, "…that whosoever looketh on a woman to lust after her hath committed adultery with her already in his heart" (Matthew 5:28).

***

He wanted to preach this wonderful teaching to everyone. He was open to giving this wonderful truth that came through him to everyone. He wanted to share it with everyone.

But the more he tried to tell people about this beautiful revelation, the more they wanted favors. They wanted to be healed. They wanted to be given whatever they wanted, and they wanted to hear what they wanted to hear.

Also, many say that they have to listen to energy, instead of listening to God. They say, "If it feels good to me, it is OK. If it does not feel good to me, it is not OK." That is a trip. That is an ego trick. "If it is according to what I want, it is OK. If it is not according to what I want, it is no good, I can drop it and go somewhere else."

So what happened? He had no choice but to give this truth to his disciples only. He went to the mountains, he sat there, and his disciples came there. There was no multitude with them at this point.

That is when he really went to the essence of his teaching, to the very depth of his teaching. That is why chapters 5, 6, and 7 of Matthew in the Bible are such wonderful chapters. The Sermon on the Mount is probably the most famous sermon by the Christ:

Blessed are the poor in spirit: for theirs is the kingdom of heaven. (Matthew 5:3)

The poor in spirit refers to those refined Souls who hate evildoings and false teachings ("deeds of the Nicolaitanes," Revelation 2:6). They intuitively know that there is more in life than only physiological satisfaction, safety needs, and pursuance of Maya (worldly attraction).

Therefore, they long for that lasting happiness. They will come to the conclusion that the Kingdom of Heaven is only within. So they forsake the society and try to find the Kingdom of Heaven within. They become escapists. That is why people will call them poor in spirit, because they do not have the courage to face hardship. So they inherit the Kingdom of Heaven within only.

Blessed are they that mourn: for they shall be comforted. (Matthew 5:4)

(☯) Those poor in spirit who have overcome being escapists and instead try to stay in society – "thy first love" (Revelation 2:4) – are those who mourn. They are poor in spirit, hate evildoings and false teachings, and they see so much wrongdoing and inequity in society. So they mourn over being oppressed in that environment and are very unhappy as to why they do not receive their fair share. They shall be comforted when the Kingdom Of Heaven On Earth comes and they will receive their fair share.

Blessed are the meek: for they shall inherit the earth. (Matthew 5:5)

(✡) When a person mourns for a while and no one listens to him, he realizes that he is too powerless to be able to gain whatever he wants. So he starts to conform instead of mourn. He becomes a meek person; he becomes submissive. He will endure suffering with patience and without resentment.
However, these are the first people who will submit themselves when the Kingdom of Heaven comes, and because they consist of the majority of the people, they will inherit the earth.

Blessed are they which do hunger and thirst after righteousness: for they shall be filled. (Matthew 5:6)

(✝) A meek person, however, after being submissive for some time, will realize that the reason for all his and others' suffering is the lack of righteousness in all levels of society. That is when he will create a strong desire for righteousness. He hungers and thirsts for righteousness to be established. These are the ones who will be filled when the Kingdom Of Heaven On Earth is established and righteousness restored.

Blessed are the merciful: for they shall obtain mercy. (Matthew 5:7)

(☪) If a person progresses more in understanding himself (overcoming the false ego), he will realize that in all the last four stages, he has been following the demands of his own false ego. He was unhappy about society and was trying to change it because he wanted a fair share for himself.
He had been in his first three chakras, which are related to the false ego. However, when he overcomes being selfish about what he wants himself, then he creates a great compassion for those in distress. He realizes that overcoming ego is a hard thing, so he creates compassion for those who are lost because of their false egos. He becomes merciful. So he himself will obtain mercy from heaven.

Blessed are the pure in heart: for they shall see God. (Matthew 5:8)

(✺) A pure in heart person is one whose innermost character, feelings, and inclinations are free from moral fault or guilt. He is a man after God's own Heart. He is a man who not only is merciful, but has created a universal point of view with utmost compassion for all things, so he looks at the universe exactly the way God looks at it. Therefore, he will start to understand how God feels about all things in His universe, and he can see God face-to-face in all the manifested universe.

Blessed are the peacemakers: for they shall be called the children of God. (Matthew 5:9)

(✡) A peacemaker is one who brings harmony, tranquility, or quietness to people internally and externally. These are the ones who not only have reached the state of being pure in heart, but are actively engaged in establishing the Kingdom Of Heaven On Earth (establishing daharma) in order to bring that harmony and tranquility to the world. They are the real Paravipras, who with their spiritual understanding and powers, bring the Kingdom Of Heaven On Earth. They are the children of God, because they have completely realized His Will and are trying to fulfill it. They are good children of God.

Blessed are they which are persecuted for righteousness' sake: for theirs is the kingdom of heaven. (Matthew 5:10)

(✺) These are the ones who have already reached a very high consciousness or Pure Consciousness and have come back to earth in order to establish the righteousness. They have no interest in this external material world for any selfish desires, but are interested in the establishment of the Kingdom Of Heaven On Earth in order to see that the proper environment is created for all to progress physically, mentally, and spiritually. They have no fear of being persecuted for their ideology and goal, because they know eternal life is everlasting and forever.

Theirs is the Kingdom of Heaven (within and without), because these are the ones who are really worthy to assume the leadership of humanity. They will be the Great Paravipras (Maha-Paravipras) who will establish and maintain the Kingdom Of Heaven On Earth.

In reality the teaching of Esa finishes here. The rest of chapter 5 is the description of the characteristics of a Paravipra.

***

He gave his message and was released from his duty to let the people know what the message of the Lord was, so it will be done – they could accept it or reject it; it was up to them now.

That is the duty of a Messenger – to give the message to those he is chosen to take it to. He is not responsible for the consequences. It is up to God.

In truth his mission as Messenger is finished here. But he should have continued until he was crucified on the cross. So he stayed and taught further, and he pressed the elders until they would do His Will.

***

Christ finished the essence of his teachings here and people saw the authority in him because he was in truth. Whoever is in truth cannot say anything but the truth, and truth is like a very sharp sword which cuts through the falsifications and prevails strongly, "having authority." But people still thought it was his doctrine and could not see that it is the **only** doctrine, or the truth. No one will be saved by merely believing in a Savior – after believing in the Savior, one has to do and struggle in the path. Then he might earn His Grace and be saved.

***

BEING BAPTIZED WITH

THE HOLY GHOST (SATVA-RAJA, OR FIRE)

IS THE ONLY TRUE WAY

OF BEING BAPTIZED.

Baptism by water is a symbol of that kind of baptism, because only after repentance and changing the way of life toward purification will a person receive The Holy Ghost and truly be baptized.

***

Water is the symbol of manifested consciousness (ether), and restless water, such as a river or ocean, is the symbol of confused consciousness or mind. Therefore to baptize in the river by letting the person merge in it, and then taking him out, is a symbol of saving the person from confusion (river) and pulling him out like a fish. That is why Christ told his disciples that he was going to make them fishers of men.

***

The feeling of bliss which accompanies baptism arises because when a person is suddenly immersed in water and then taken out again, the reaction to this act is the release of some prana from the solar plexus to the brain.

Also, because the chakras become cooled, they will be quickened. Both of these reactions result in a feeling of bliss and refreshment, which is interpreted as receiving the Spirit and being saved. This feeling is intensified with a religious atmosphere which stimulates the emotions.

In truth, all of these result in the quickening of the chakras, which is the same as receiving the Spirit (awakening the astral body). However, only those who truly repent, overcome the lower nature, and go to their higher natures (to be born again) are the true saved ones.

***

Esa taught that you have to be born again. To be born again means to go from the first three chakras (lower nature) to the higher chakras (higher self), or in other words, to crucify the false ego (lower self) so to be born again (resurrect) into the higher self and be glorified. That is why until you are born again, you are not saved. In fact the very symbolic meaning of the crucifixion of Esa (symbol of the death of the false ego) and his resurrection is to show that you have to die first (your false ego) before you can be born again (resurrect to the higher self), "It is in dying that we are born to Eternal Life" (St. Francis of Assisi).

***

Christianity is the symbol of this overcoming of these first three chakras. It is a symbol of individual achievement in detaching completely from Maya. He who overcomes the first three chakras overcomes evil (attraction of Maya), and is a true disciple of Christ.

***

Consciousness in its purest form is "The magical world of God." To enter this state many techniques have been devised. The fastest and the most direct of all is the path of devotion to God. That is why Esa said, "Love thy Lord with all your Heart, Mind, and Being." When you create such an intense Love of God, the Fire of this devotion will burn all impurities (tama guna). That is when one will reach the ecstasy of God-realization.

***

Esa Came As A Universal Personality With A Teaching Of Equality.

He came with "balances in his hand" (Revelation 6:5). He was, as a symbol, the first of the Jews who truly overcame his lower nature or false ego, "…and lo a black horse; and he that sat on him…" (Revelation 6:5).

***

(יהושוה) was the faithful witness because he came and struggled to bring humanity to higher consciousness and Pure Consciousness. He was the "first begotten of the dead," or he was the first that came from ignorance to complete enlightenment. So he was the first one that reached Pure Consciousness and he became The First Begotten Son. He was begotten from the dead, which means ignorance. He was "the prince of the kings of the earth," which means that he is the ruler of the earth. The real kingdom of the earth has been given to him.

"He washed us from our sins in his own blood," or he washed the sins of others by sacrificing himself, because he took up the struggle through the crucifixion and through showing how we can wash our sins through sacrificing to establish the Kingdom of Heaven. With the fire of sacrifice we can purify the world.

***

He who has the pair of balances has come to make sure that equity has been established in the human race.

Whosoever contributes more to society should receive more. Spiritual contribution is superior to intellectual, and intellectual contribution is superior to physical. Another meaning is that the chosen ones (Paravipras) will establish this equity on earth. These are the ones that have the pair of balances in themselves (Kingdom Of Heaven Within).

In short, "Make sure all receive their share without any one being unfairly treated." That is what Christ taught his disciples. The essence of his teachings is, "Sacrifice in establishing the Kingdom of Heaven." The rest will be added to you.

***

The Miracles

Esa Himself

Did Not Want To Make People

Believe In Him

Because Of His Miracles,

But Because Of

His Teachings.

However, in order to make people believe in him, miracles were used. As history has shown, **people become so attached to the miracles of the Prophet that they forget about the teachings**. Miracles are for those who do not understand the reason behind how they are manifested. For he who knows the Laws behind all things, there is no miracle, and all things are miracles!

***

Christ knew that the only way to make people in that era and level of consciousness believe in him was by healing them and performing miracles. But for the people of this time and of the era to come, the teachings of the Prophets should become more important than the Prophets themselves, or their miracles. Each man has to learn to heal himself.

It was not important for Christ that he healed the people. Instead, he desired to see that the people would follow the Laws and glorify the Father. He did great actions but took no pride for them, because it is He who did these through him.

***

He taught the teachings of the Kingdom to his disciples, not to the people, because the multitudes were only interested in favors and miracles, not the truth.

***

Instead of meditating on and contemplating the evidence that the coming of the Messiah was imminent, and then listening to Esa's teachings and seeing the truth behind them, the people were resisting him and the truth he had brought. Even with all his miracles and truth he taught, they still wanted more evidence. In reality most humans do not want to hear the truth. Many love darkness, because the Light blinds them.

***

Christ looked and saw how people were lost like sheep with no shepherd. But he was alone and few could understand him, and even fewer were able to depart and teach the truth he was trying to spread. That is why he felt such a compassion toward the people who needed to be guided, yet very few could do that, "the laborers are few."

That is why humanity should have waited, so that through many lifetimes of progress there would be more laborers ready to guide others to the truth, "that he will send forth laborers into his harvest." The harvest time is **NOW**. Many laborers will be ready to guide the sheep to the goal of the life.

***

HISTORY HAS SHOWN

THAT MIRACLES

DO NOT MAKE

BETTER BELIEVERS.

The **Mission of Maitreya** blends everything into it and dissolves it into ourselves so it becomes one with us instead of opposing it. It just becomes one with the energy.

For example, the Hindu religion is so powerful that if you really understand it, then you understand other Scriptures. If you do not know about the Mystical Paths, when you read the Bible, it is very hard to explain. When Christ said, "Take your bed and go home," everyone wonders what he meant. Or he said, "Your sins are forgiven, now you are healed," and everyone says, "It is very hard to see the relationship between forgiving sin and being healed."

But if you know the Law of Karma and Samskaras, that our diseases and our problems are mostly related to our previous lifetimes and the sins and karma we created, and because of that this person is blind, or this person cannot walk, then when we read the Bible and it says, "You can walk because your sins are forgiven," you can completely understand what Christ was talking about.

He was talking about, your karma is taken away from you. You do not have any karma anymore. So you do not have to have disease any longer. So the man took his bed and went home.

Of course, Christ realized later on that if he healed other people, they would not learn how to heal themselves. Hence, he said, "When the unclean spirit goes out of the body, it goes and finds seven more and says, 'Hey, the house is clean, let us go back,' and the state of the person is worse than it was before." Still the person was the same person. He did not know how to heal himself. If he knew, Christ would not have had to heal him. That is why the state of the person became worse than it was before.

Now, we are trying to teach every person to heal himself. If you learn how to heal yourself, when that spirit goes out, it cannot say, "The house is empty, we can go and find seven more and go back." If you are able to force the first one out, you can force the seven others out too.

That is why we are not preaching very much about the healing that a lot of people are either doing, or are after. A couple of healers came to the **Mission** and talked about the people they had healed, and later on these people because worse because they did not know how to do it themselves.

As long as you do not know how to do it, that spirit is going to come back. Maybe that spirit is afraid of me, but he is not afraid of you. It is going to come back later on with even greater force. So that does not work.

***

Also as long as a sick person does not believe he is sick, he does not go to the doctor. But when he realizes he is sick, then he seeks medical care. That is also true about the human. As long as they think they are not sinners (are not ignorant), they do not feel they need a Savior who can take them away from ignorance to the Light (knowledge).

That is why the publicans and sinners went to Christ to hear his words, but the scribes and Pharisees who also were ignorant but unaware of it, did not go to him. They had created a big false ego so they could not see the Light in Christ.

Also, many would do much sacrifice and go through different penances, but did not have any mercy toward other humans. That is why Christ said, "I will have mercy, and not sacrifice." That is, the goal of sacrifice and penance, etc., is to become merciful toward the lost souls and try to help them out of ignorance, not to forsake the society and become an escapist.

***

A lot of people want someone to heal them. They do not want to learn how to heal themselves. They do not want to learn their lessons.

That is why we are here, to learn our lessons. If we do not learn our lessons, what good is it to be healed for a month, or two, or three months, and later we become even worse than we were before? That is why I say, "You have to learn to heal yourself."

That is the healing power of the Golden Age. In the Golden Age, the age coming, we will increase our understanding of how our bodies, how our minds, how this energy works. Because we will understand, and because we will create the ability to deal with this karmic energy, the unclean spirits will not be able to affect us. So we can free ourselves from this burden, this negativity.

***

Well, if I can heal, so can you. If Esa could heal a lot of people, so could those people heal themselves. One of the problems with one person healing another person is, the person who heals opens the aura of the other person and forces the impurity out of it. The person who is healed did not learn anything. Also, because their auras are opened, even greater impurities might enter later on ("seven more spirits").

However, if they can learn how to heal themselves, then they can block the negativity from themselves, and we will have much healthier and happier people rather than a few people being burdened to heal many. And that is why in this lifetime we are trying **to heal the earth instead of healing individuals**.

***

You want miracles? Look at your hand. Miracles are everywhere – a miracle is happening every moment. Just look at the birth of a child. That is a miracle. The entire body of a woman is completely transformed, and she is changed hormonally just to create that child. Who knows what hormone needs to be in what time period of the birth to make the child come to that certain stage? How does the body know that when you are 14 or 15 years old it is the time for puberty?

There is something there that creates all this. You say it is genetic but there is a Spirit behind genes that does that. Genes are just a mathematical equation that is created with the Greater Mind. Genes are a computer program. But there should be a programmer behind the program itself. So look at these miracles. Miracles are the simplest things. And God is in the simplest things in life.

***

A true believer sees miracles all around himself or herself. Such a person looks at his hands, eyes, others, nature, the events in his life, universe, etc. and sees all as a miracle from God. These are sufficient for the true believers.

Other miracles, such as healing, which are sought by many, are miracles to them because they do not know the principles behind them. If they become a channel for God, these miracles are the birthright of every individual.

***

As the consciousness of the human rises, there will be fewer demands for miracles and emphasis will be more on teaching and understanding the realities of the spiritual world. In the past, many miracles were shown in order to awaken the low consciousness of the regular humans and to develop belief in an Unseen Power. However, the human with a higher consciousness in this age does not need to be shown miracles. He can look at his body, universe, and all things, and see the Hand of the Invisible Power.

Also, people usually put their attention on the miracles performed by the Prophet or on his personality, and they forget the true teaching and depth of his Revelations. That is why those who are ready for the realization of the truth behind the realities of the spiritual world do not need miracles, and those who will not believe, will not believe even after they are shown the miracles, as it has happened in the past. Listen to His Voice in your Heart!

***

THE FULFILLMENT

Every Prophet Comes To Continue
To Fulfill His Will.
They Come Not To Destroy Other Teachings,
Or Other Prophets, Or Other Messiahs,
But To Continually Push The Will Of God
To Be Fulfilled On Earth.
The Ultimate Manifestation Of This Process Is
The Coming Of The Seventh Angel.

We know that there have been seven Prophets, seven Messiahs, or seven teachers. Each of these seven Messengers came one after another to further purify, fulfill, and advance God's Will to Its ultimate fulfillment, which is to realize all the Seven Seals on earth and all the prophecies and wonders that God has sent us, and bring His Kingdom on earth.

We are doing the same thing. We are not here to destroy anything but to fulfill, to advance, to bring God's Will to earth more and more, and to bring His Kingdom to humanity. The Messiah never comes to destroy. He comes to destroy what is not the Will of God.

***

That is what every Prophet comes to do, to fulfill the Will of God. The Will of God has already been prophesied. How He is going to do it can be read all through the <u>Bible</u>. He told Abraham how he had to leave his parents, his house, and the land he was living in, and go somewhere else. With that He promised He would bless him and bless his children.

You know the story about Abraham's two sons. God promised that there would be a Messiah, a Prophet, a Messenger from each of them, and each of them was going to have a kingdom, a status in the spiritual world. He fulfilled all of His Promises.

***

The people were asking for signs instead of listening to Esa's teachings and truth. Many signs were given before by many Prophets and still people did not believe in them, listen to their words, or follow the truths they revealed. Esa came, performed many miracles, and taught them the truth, but still they were asking for signs. The false ego seeks all kinds of excuses to not see the truth.

However, the only sign he gave them was "the sign of prophet Jonas."

This was the only sign he gave them to witness as the sign of his authority. But even this sign has been distorted by the paganizers of Christianity in the Roman Empire, after Christianity was accepted as the state religion.

It is believed that he was crucified on Friday and rose on Sunday. However, study of the gospels shows that Christ was put in the cave ("heart of the earth") in the evening. According to the belief of the majority, he was in the cave Friday night, Saturday during the day and Saturday night, and rose on Sunday morning. This would mean that he was in the "heart of the earth" only two nights and one day. So if we believe this (that he died on Friday night and rose Sunday morning), then Esa failed to fulfill the only sign he gave for his legitimacy.

However, if he had been crucified on Friday and stayed in the cave for "three days and three nights," then he should have risen on Monday afternoon about the same time of day that he had been put into the earth.

The truth is that Mary and her companions went to the cave where Esa was laid on that Sunday morning and found it empty. That is because he had left it the evening before, on Saturday afternoon, around the same time when he was put inside the cave on the day he was crucified (later than the ninth hour of the day or three o'clock in the afternoon by our time standard). Therefore, he was taken to the cave on the Wednesday before that Saturday and he was in the "heart of the earth for three days and three nights." That is why those women who went to the cave the next Sunday morning did not find him there.

So, he fulfilled his promise of staying in the heart of the earth for three nights and three days by being in the cave from Wednesday until Saturday afternoon, the Sabbath.

This truth, like many other truths about Christ and his teaching, was changed after Christianity became the state religion of the Romans, with acceptance by the masses in great multitudes. They accepted the basic concepts of Christianity with Christ as the Savior, but they transformed it into a new religion with many flavors of their pagan religions, especially Mithraism.

In fact, it was a part of the doctrine of Mithraism that a Savior from a virgin would come and all would be saved through him. So this part of the story of the birth of Christ matched their basic beliefs. Also they injected their own festivals and holidays into the new religion. That is why most of the Christian religious holidays have pagan origins from the Roman religions.

Sunday was the weekly holiday in which the sun god (Mithra) was worshipped, and Friday also was an exalted day. That is why a formula was created so that both Friday and Sunday stayed exalted as before. Indeed the true Christians of the east and far west in England observed Hebrew Holy days (their list is in Leviticus 23 in the <u>Bible</u>) until 700 A.D., and their Sabbath was on Saturday.

***

After Esa established the supremacy of his teachings and actions over those of the Pharisees, scribes, and Sadducees, and silenced them, then he started his direct attack and the last part of his mission to show their hypocrisy. He did not speak in parables any longer but in plain language. This would do the last hurting to the false egos of the priests, elders, and spiritual teachers of the people, and would make them more zealous to plot against him. Although he said the truth, they did not want to hear it.

He was trying to show that it is not the teaching of Moses which is bad or should not be followed, but it was the actions of their leaders which had corrupted Moses' teachings and laws. That is why what they said, which is what Moses taught, was good for a person and his spirit. But they themselves did not follow what Moses taught, "for they say, and do not."

Again this shows that Christ did not come to do away with God's Commandments and Laws. His mission was something else and he fulfilled them all.

***

Everything happened in Esa's life so that the prophecies would be fulfilled and Esa, as an Avatar (Emmanuel, "God with us," god-man), would be born. Again God showed that He never fails to fulfill His Promises, and that all the prophecies eventually will be fulfilled. Humanity must and will realize that the best way is His Way, and the goal and purpose of this creation is that all reach Pure Consciousness.

***

THE DUTY OF A PROPHET OR MESSENGER

IS TO GIVE THE MESSAGE;

HE IS NOT RESPONSIBLE

IF PEOPLE ACCEPT IT OR NOT!

Many believed Esa and it seemed to the priests that he was going to destroy their already established, quiet social structures. That is why they not only rejected him but put him on the cross without a cause. That was a great sin.

However, no man can stop God's Plan. Even with putting Esa on the cross, the new teaching could not be completely suppressed and Christianity flourished.

***

Hebrews were selected to establish the Kingdom Of Heaven On Earth. But they failed in their mission. However, they should have failed because other truths in **The Greatest Sign** should have been revealed and many prophecies should have been fulfilled before the true Kingdom of Heaven would come. A part of them became an example for humanity throughout history to show that whenever any person or group fails, they are punished. After punishment, when they are purified, they are given another chance to prove themselves worthy. After they fail again, they create bad karma and are punished to be purified once more. The example of the Jewish race should be a lesson for all of humanity and shows how the Law of Karma works collectively and also individually.

***

Christ fulfilled his mission even if it appears that the Jews did not accept him. But God keeps His Promises in ways that humans cannot understand easily. The reason is very simple: Because humans do not look at His universe as He sees it. He has a complete picture of everything and is guiding the whole universe toward its goal.

***

This truth has been said many, many times and has come to humanity many, many times. So the more we reveal this truth and people see it, accept it, and embrace it, the better communities we are going to have, the better people we are going to have, and the better earth we are going to have. Eventually, after a certain percentage of humanity accepts this, the rest will easily come to terms with this truth and we will have the Kingdom Of Heaven On Earth.

So we can see that people who resist a new revelation or teaching should not do that, because when any teaching, any Prophet, or the Messiah comes, it is not to destroy anything. They come to fulfill, they come to bring a greater beauty to humanity. They do not come to oppose.

Actually, humanity opposes the revelation, or the teacher, because they want to keep their own ways. They want to resist His Way, God's Ways, even to the point where they kill the Messiah. Christ was crucified, Muhammad was stoned, Bab was executed, etc. Even the Prophets of the Old Testament went through much struggle to convey the Will of God.

***

In the garden of Gethsemane, Esa (Jesus) did not really want to go through the last stage, the crucifixion! He said to God, "May you take this cup from me? I do not want to go through with it." That was not submission. "Thy Will, not mine," is submission. But he went through it anyway. That is why when he came back the next lifetime, he brought the teaching of submission and surrendering. He learned a little more about God's Ways.

Of course, his mission was completely different then. Each time the Messiah comes he has a different mission to perform. However, people usually realize his station after he is gone. That is why after they killed Esa, then people started loving him and being so devotional toward him.

***

You have to surrender yourself to the words revealed through the Prophets and follow them. The Prophet himself is important only because of what he says. So those who put more importance on the Prophet himself than on his words, which are from God, miss the whole point. They will call him "Lord, Lord," but forget to follow what he said. Such people will not enter into heaven or the Kingdom Of God In Heaven, because they have not purified themselves by following his teachings and still have big false egos. Whoever has the slightest false ego cannot enter into heaven.

***

Anytime

A New Revelation

Comes To Earth,

Many Are Guided

And Many Others

Will Go Astray.

John taught that Christ would come to separate the good and bad, and judge between them in truth. He is the light and the truth. Those who were ready would be attracted to him and those who were not ready would be blinded by it and go far astray.

***

Whenever the Messiah comes, he differentiates between the chaff and the wheat. That is the prophecy. If you believe in the prophecies, all through the prophecies it has always been suggested that the chaff will be separated from the wheat when the Messiah comes. The person who has been prophesied to come will do that. So whatever the Messiah or this Chosen Person says, is the wheat, and whatever is not according to the wheat, is the chaff. It is very simple.

***

Even Christ knew about **The Greatest Sign** 2,000 years ago. He was saying the same thing: First you start awakening your spiritual forces, then you want to create an environment where they give you your fair share, then you sacrifice, then you become submissive, a universalist, pure in heart, and eventually you become a Paravipra. The Paravipra is the peacemaker, the person who wants to create the **Communities of Light** and the Kingdom Of Heaven On Earth.

That is how peace comes to earth. At the same time there are peacemakers in the **Communities of Light** too. They want to bring harmony and oneness in the community.

So we can see the relationship between Christ's teaching and **The Greatest Sign**. By going to the sixth chakra you become a peacemaker, you become a Paravipra. You go beyond mourning. You become mature.

When you are mature, you are no longer poor in spirit. You no longer mourn. You are no longer meek. You long for righteousness, but at the same time you are pure in heart. You have compassion for other people. You are pure in heart; you see God in everything, and because of that you can bring peace to others.

Then you are a leader. You are a person who can create **Communities of Light**, who can see the plight of other people. You do not want to be understood anymore. You understand.

Why do you want to be understood? The only person you really have to be concerned to understand you is yourself. If you understand yourself, you do not need to be understood. If you understand yourself, you understand God. Isn't that it? Know thyself to know God.

Understand yourself. Understand God. When you understand God, you become effective, you become a peacemaker. You no longer need to be understood. If you understand yourself, who cares if anyone else understands you? You understand yourself. So you become a peacemaker.

***

You start from the I-Ching in the horizontal position (☯). Horizontal means not awakened. By spiritual practices you awaken your spiritual forces. Then you try to create the **Communities**

of Light (✡), to establish the Kingdom Of Heaven On Earth. In order to create the **Communities of Light**, not being self-centered, or sacrifice, is necessary (✝). Even after sacrificing, you might become attached to your sacrifice. That is when submission (☾) comes in. You sacrifice, yet it is really God who is doing it through you; you are not the doer.

After being submissive, you become a Universalist (✹); God is the universe. When you go through these five steps, you become an Elect (✡), a Paravipra. Such are the people who will help the whole universe to reach Pure Consciousness. They themselves also reached Pure Consciousness (✺), or are in the image of God, and they know the Will of God.

***

If your Soul and your Spirit understand that **The Goal Of The Life Is To Be(come) Divine, That Divinity (God) Is Everything**, and that the way to create peace and tranquility on earth is the **Communities of Light** and establishing the Kingdom Of Heaven On Earth, then you are a Child of Light, an Elect.

***

Who has been persecuted? Wasn't Noah persecuted, and Abram (Abraham), Moses, Muhammad, and Christ? Even King David was persecuted for a while. He ran away and eventually returned and became King.

Who else was persecuted? Weren't the disciples of Christ persecuted? The disciples of Muhammad were persecuted. The disciples of Bab were persecuted. The people who followed Noah were persecuted.

Blessed are they, because they will inherit the Kingdom. They have been chosen to inherit the Kingdom. They are the channels of God. Who would be better to inherit the Kingdom than the people who are the channels for God?

Their efforts were not wasted. Any lifetime they came, they were persecuted. They had a hard time. But each time they came, they gathered a few more people who would listen to them. So their numbers increased and increased and increased.

***

Why will Christ and his followers be preferred to the disbelievers? Because he and his followers were always preferred to disbelievers. They are the Elected Ones. The people who followed Christ were Elected Ones, as the people who followed Prophet Muhammad were Elected Ones.

These people have been reincarnated again and again, and each time they set the world in the right direction. After they leave, in a short period of time, humanity becomes corrupt again. So they have to come back. Each time they come back, however, some new people will be saved and reach higher consciousness. This process will continue until all understand The Plan of God and establish the Kingdom Of Heaven On Earth. That is why Christ called them "the salt of the earth."

Without these people, we would not even be here where we are now. That is why they are above disbelievers. They are the Elected Ones, the Divines.

***

  Paravipras can be related to the last three stages of progress in **The Greatest Sign**: Those who reach the sixth stage in **The Greatest Sign** (✡), those who reach the seventh stage (✿), but do not leave their bodies in order to help others reach Pure Consciousness (men-gods or Satgurus), and those who have reached Pure Consciousness (✿) but will return to help others reach Pure Consciousness (god-men or Avatars). However, we can say the last two are Maha-Paravipras (Great Paravipras). With these Great Paravipras, other Paravipras, and His First Begotten Son, God will bring His Kingdom on earth (Daharma).
  His Will, will be done on earth as it is in heaven.

***

IN THE BEGINNING
OF THE SPREAD OF CHRISTIANITY,
THE FOLLOWERS OF ESA
OBSERVED GOD'S HOLY DAYS,
BUT AFTER THE ROMANS
ACCEPTED CHRISTIANITY,
THEIR PAGAN HOLIDAYS WERE CHRISTIANIZED.

After Christianity started to flourish and was accepted by the Elected Ones, its followers were persecuted because of its depth, truth, and being against the worldly interests of many. But it could not be stopped, because of the vigorous preaching of the true gospel by Christ's disciples and their willingness to sacrifice all things for their ideology.

So, many churches were founded, and with the great struggle by Christ's disciples and many others, the seed of Christianity was planted.

However, as it is revealed in the books after the four gospels in the Bible (Acts, Romans, etc.) from the very beginning many false teachers wished to influence Christ's teachings in one way or another (Acts 8:1-24, Jude 1:4). The apostles fought vigorously with these influences and somehow established a pure ideology of Christ's teachings.

These true teachings lasted about 400 years, until Christianity was accepted by Rome's emperors and then by the majority of the people.

Thousands of people started to accept Christianity as their religion. But they did not want to give up their previous beliefs completely and follow Christianity wholeheartedly. Many of these people had previously followed the worshipping of the sun-god. They had many pagan ideas, festivals, holidays, etc., but their religions lacked the universal outlook. They believed in the sun-god, but Christians believed in the Father, the universal, invisible God who had complete power over the whole universe, even over the sun.

Also the concept of Christ as being born from a virgin mother (which he was) fit into the belief of the followers of Mithra (sun-god of Zoroastrians) that Mithra would be born from a virgin to save the world. Many of the Romans were followers of Mithra.

With all these factors presented, and also because of the freedom-loving and democratic ideals of the Romans, people were left to make anything they wanted out of Christianity.

The sun-god was replaced by the son of God. The Virgin Mary took the place of the Virgin Mother. The Saturday Sabbath was changed to Sunday (their day of worshipping the sun), and God's festivals (revealed in chapter 23 of Leviticus in the Bible as Holy Days to keep for ever and ever) were replaced with pagan festivals (refer to encyclopedias about the origin of Christian festivals). In fact, Passover, the Feast of Tabernacles, and other Holy Days of God were observed by the apostles and many of their followers until about 700 A.D. Many other things were changed which cannot be found in the Bible but are now followed by many.

However, those who were to be saved by Christ were saved in the first 400 years of Christianity. Those who had not been saved eventually will be after many lifetimes or in future creations.

This is, however, a historical explanation. These happenings were revealed many centuries before they occurred in the prophecies in the book of Daniel (the dream of King Nebuchadnezzar, the vision of the four beasts, and the vision of the ram and the he goat), and in The Revelation (the third church, Revelation 2:12-16).

In the visions of Daniel, the little horn, which is the symbol of the intellectualization of things, is prophesied to change the true religions, "the same ... made war with the saints" (Daniel 7:21), and to try to replace the truth by believing that the intellect of man is superior to all things (read Commentaries on Prophecies in Daniel, Period of Intellectual Domination in **THOTH**).

Also, in The Revelation, the last book of the Bible, in the message to the third church (which is the third sign in **The Greatest Sign**, the cross), it is revealed that in this church there are still some who "hold the doctrine of Balaam,…" (Revelation 2:14). The "doctrine of Balaam" is the pagan ideas and festivals which entered into this third church.

So God had revealed many centuries before what will happen in the future. Now it is time for the human to see the limits of his intellect and understandings, then surrender himself to God and the words revealed through His Prophets, and overcome the confusion between them by understanding **The Greatest Sign**. Then the Glory of God will be realized and His Kingdom will come on earth as it is in heaven.

***

Actually the first Christians celebrated the Holy Days of God for 700 years, until Christianity became accepted by the Roman Empire. The Romans were sun worshippers. Even their hairstyle was like the sun. And they had a god for every element in the universe.

So, the return of the sun became the birthday of the Son of God (equinox), which is not the truth, because Esa was not born at this time. As we remember, the shepherds were in the mountains with their sheep then. In the East, people do not keep their sheep out in the desert in such cold weather. They usually put them in special stables to keep them warm during the winter. The weather should have been pretty nice and warm that they had their sheep with them in the mountains. So most probably Esa was born either in the spring or late in the summer or fall. There is no way that he was born at this time of year.

And I do not think he ever talked about Santa Claus either. Some of these ideas come from North Europe, like Santa Claus comes from North Europe, because they receive less and less daylight. Actually they reach a point where the nights are very long and the days are very short. So the return of the long days (sun) was celebrated. Most of the ideas of Santa Claus living in the North Pole and these myths came from the northern part of Europe.

About having a white Christmas – well, we are not having a white Christmas here. It is pretty dry here. These ideas all came from northern Europe, which always has snow this time of year. So if we make the people think about it, then they will realize this holiday is not really related to any spiritual significance. It is all man-made.

But because we are so engrossed in our tradition, our country, or our religion, our concepts are so narrow that we cannot let go of them. "Oh, you mean we are not going to celebrate Christmas? We are not going to give presents? Or we are not going to put ornaments on the trees? It is such an awful thing, we cannot even think about not doing that."

They had the same type of celebrations in the culture I came from. They did not celebrate Christmas but they had something similar. However, in order to create unity for humanity, in order to bring God into our midst, we have to let our traditions, our concepts, and our narrow views go. We have to completely eradicate those kinds of feelings, go beyond them and say, "OK, I know where they come from, I have to forego them and I have to follow God, because that is the Will of God."

***

When the religion becomes dogma, what happens? That **Message** dies. The dead body is going to be lying there but the followers will just be clinging to the dead body and saying, "Oh, no. Our body has been fragmented into many different sects and religions and denominations, and every denomination or sect says, 'I have the answer.'"

How many denominations do we have in Christianity? At this time, we have 2,000 and some. How many sects do we have in the Jewish religion? How many do we have in Islam? We have the Shi'ites. We have the Sunnis, Hanaphies, Ishmaelites, etc. How many do we have in Hinduism or in the Baha'i Faith? Even the Baha'is split in the 1970s. And there are still the Babis in the Middle East who follow the Bab instead of Bahá'u'lláh. They say Bab was the Prophet, not Bahá'u'lláh.

So we say, "Which one is right, which sect is right?" Is the **Mission of Maitreya** also going to split into many sects and different denominations? Again, we have the opportunity to not let it happen. It could, but we have to take the opportunity to stop it.

***

Then again, either they have to celebrate the Messiah's birthday as he came again and again, or they have to say, "We do not want to celebrate the Prophet's birthday, we want to celebrate God's Holy Days." Then they have to forego birthday celebrations. If they want to follow God's Will, God says, "These are my Holy Days, you keep them Holy forever." Then they will forget about their birthdays, holidays, and Prophet's birthdays, and they will keep the Holy Days of God.

***

Collective thought can exist. For instance, everyone who believes that "Christ is the only way," creates a concept of his own. This collective belief or thought creates a religion. We have collective thoughts of those who live in a nation, race, philosophy, etc. Each of them create their own collective thought form. These are sub-collective thought forms to the Universal Thought Form.

The greatest thought form is the Universal Thought Form. God is Thought Form, which is the lower creation to His Highest Ideal. Any other subliminal thought forms are still separate from this Universal Thought Form. When you expand yourself to realize His Thought Form, these other small groups or collective forms are dissolved.

It is like the vision Arjuna had of Krishna in His Universal Form. God was unaffected, a witness entity to His creation, which are His Thought Forms, but Arjuna could not bear such a vast drama of creation being created, destroyed, etc.

So do not be trapped in small groups or subliminal thought forms. Realize God in His Fullest.

***

The Return

As God Has Declared In The Book Of The Revelation (The Last Book In The Bible), His Work Will Remain A Mystery Until The Time Of The Seventh Angel.

But in the days of the voice of the seventh angel, ... the mystery of God should be finished,.... (Revelation 10:7)

***

Two thousand years ago, when Christ was on earth, He taught a prayer, "Thy kingdom come, Thy will be done on earth as it is in heaven…" We now have given the fulfillment of that prayer. As you see in the prayer, it does not say, "Your Kingdom come in heaven." It is already established there. And it does not say, "Your Kingdom come within us," which He also preached, "The Kingdom of Heaven is within you," somewhere else in the Scriptures.

The emphasis is also that His Kingdom comes on earth: On earth – the whole earth – not on only a portion of the earth.

***

God wants to be the King. There should be a focus to unify all to His Kingdom. So that is why the question of the Messiah, or the coming of the King, or the coming of the Promised One comes in. If you realize the Kingdom of Heaven within you, and you realize that God is the King of the universe, then you are close to His Will. And if you are close to His Will, then you realize that His Will has come through **The Greatest Sign**, through **THOTH**, and through the **Mission**. With this realization you will see who **Maitreya** is, who the Messiah is, who the Promised One is.

***

If you look at the Scriptures you will see, in the <u>Bhagavad-Gita</u>, in the <u>Puranas</u>, in the <u>Koran</u>, in the Buddhist teaching, in the Christian teaching, in the Jewish teaching, in the Baha'i teaching, in all the religions, they are supported by the revelations from God. And in all those religions the concept of the Messiah, in many different languages, is revealed. They all believe in a being as the Chosen One who will come to separate the chaff from the wheat. He is God manifested. God always manifests Himself on earth.

And when does He come? Look at the <u>Bhagavad-Gita</u>, which says, "Whenever morality is low and the people start going astray from God, my Spirit arises on earth in order to establish righteousness."

***

As Christ said, "You look at the day and you see it is fair and the sky is red. You know it is going to be a fair night." They asked him about the signs. They were looking for signs and miracles over and over again. He had already done many miracles but still the people were asking him about the signs.

He said, "You do not really need signs. Only the generation of vipers and the people who are not connected to God ask for signs, not the people who really want to know the truth." See, the person who is aware of his environment and of the time, by looking at the time, can see that all the signs are there that this earth needs something new. It is in bad shape. Everyone is trying to bring the Golden Age, to reach somewhere different than what has been already tried and failed. So we can see all the signs are there that humans are ready for another leap in evolution, an evolutionary leap.

All the Scriptures, if you read them, prophesy that there is going to be an end time, not in a sense that everything is going to end, but that the old era is going to finish and the Golden Era is going to approach. In every religion and every teaching you look at, they are talking about the Golden Age, a time that will come when everyone is going to connect back to God.

That is why we can look at the earth right now and see the signs that are all over. There are wars. There is strife. There are purifications. Cultures are mixing with cultures. People are not satisfied with their own religions any longer. Either they are not satisfied, or they are becoming dogmatic about them and are trying to convert other people, not with love, understanding, and bringing greater truth to them, but by buying them, fighting them, or overpowering them. The people of every religion want to convert the whole earth to their own ideology and religion.

So which religion is going to make it? Is everyone going to become Christian? Is everyone going to become Jewish, or Moslem, or Hindu? They have been here for thousands of years.

But there is religion and there is the truth. That truth is what is going to unify humanity, not religion. And all these religions that have come, according to our teaching, have a part in **The Greatest Sign**.

***

**The Only Sign
Christ Gave For
His Ultimate Return
Was That He Will Come
"In The Name Of The Lord."**

The Holy Name of the Lord (יהוה) is in him, and he (יהושוה) is in the Holy Name of the Lord. This Sacred Name of the Lord is the only name of the Lord which cannot be pronounced or uttered in the manifested (material) world. It is the Name of the Son (יהושוה), who comes in the Name of the Father (יהוה), as One, The Word (יהושוה/יהוה).

He will not be recognized (accepted) by everyone. He will be accepted only by those who recognize him and see that he is Blessed (Blessing), and they will also Bless him and will be Blessed, "Blessed is he that cometh in the name of the Lord."

***

We are now in the last phase of the fulfillment of all the karma that humanity has created over the last 12,000 years. Now is the time of complete clearance – clearing these karmas.

Of course, if everyone listened to us tomorrow, we could come together and create the Kingdom. We have brought, according to many people who read **THOTH**, "The greatest revelation that ever came to earth."

The prophecy of the teaching that will bring unity to all religions of the world is fulfilled. It has given the system to bring the Kingdom Of Heaven On Earth. Still people will not participate. They will not join because they say, "No, I have my own illusion. I have my own idea. I am a channel of this entity or I am a channel of that person. Or I have my children. I have my wife. I have my husband, my wedding, my mortgage to pay…"

It is like 2,000 years ago, when Esa said, "Come to the wedding and participate." They said, "No, we have our own things to do." They did not want to listen. They even crucified Him. Yet, could they stop His mission? No, they could not stop His mission. He went on and it manifested itself anyway.

***

Some say, "If Esa comes this time, we are going to follow him. We are not going to let him be crucified again." Here we have brought this teaching that has given all the answers and then we receive a letter, "No man has all the answers." We are not presenting a man. We are presenting the Father. We present God. God has all the answers. He knows how all this should be.

It is just like in the time of Muhammad. They looked at him as a person – he walked, he talked, he sat, he slept, he ate – so how could it be? How could he, a person, have all the answers? How could he become a Prophet of God?

Muhammad said, "God never sent any Prophet who did not speak, eat, talk, or walk." It is the same thing. We have these problems. So humans have their own concepts of all these problems. That is why they have to go through these purifications, so they come to this conclusion, "Yes, this is the answer."

***

It is now the time that the Lamb (the spirit of the truth, or the one who has reached higher consciousness, or the Christ, or the (יהושוח) who overcame the lower nature and was slain, and then knew the reality behind this universe) marries with his wife, which is the real way and the truth of higher consciousness. And, "Blessed are they which are called unto the marriage supper of the Lamb." Blessed are those who understand this truth. They will be in higher consciousness and will be called to the supper of the Lamb (which means they will be in Pure Consciousness).

The truth which comes to the earth is **the** marriage ceremony of the Lamb, because that is what Christ, the spirit of truth, the Soul of the human, wants to see established on earth. When it comes, those who have been invited to it have overcome their lower natures and are in their higher natures. These will be blessed.

***

The first step is to realize (recognize) the Messiah (יהושוח) and the second is to proclaim Him. The third step is 100% commitment to Him and His **Mission**.

When a person recognizes Him and proclaims Him, such a person accepts the greatest responsibility, which is to Be(come) One with the Body of Christ. You first realize Him with the Heart, then proclaim Him with the mouth.

It is then that a period of great testing follows. This is to see how much the Heart and mouth are One. God does not accept lukewarmness, "so then because thou art lukewarm, … I will spue thee out of my mouth" (Revelation 3:16). The Heart must be 100% One with the mouth! Such a person then is no longer a separate ego but a part of the body of the Messiah and a channel for Him (The Most High). They are One ("Not my will, but thine!").

***

Two thousand years ago, Esa came and chose twelve people. What did they do? They went out and said, "We have found the Messiah." And that was enough to build a fire that burned all throughout the earth. That is all they did, "We have found the Messiah." That is what those who are one with their Essence also have to say. They know the Kingdom within and realize this is the answer to human problems and everything that they have been praying for.

"We have found the Messiah." They do not have to go to the streets and yell, "We have found the Messiah." They would probably be put in the madhouse. They can start from their families. They can start from their friends. They can start from those people who will listen to them. They can present them the truth, present them the unification and the unifying force behind **The Greatest Sign**, behind **THOTH**, behind the teaching.

The Body is also here as a symbol of the manifestation of God's Will. You want to know His Will? That is what the Messiah is for – He comes to earth to say, "This is my Father's Will. Do it." Esa came and said, "This is what the Father wants from you." But the Jews rejected him – which was in the Plan, that was to happen, as is explained in our teachings.

So that is His Will. Have you come here to do God's Will? If you have and if you realize that our teaching is His Will, then you have a great responsibility to become a part of the Body and to proclaim Him – "Yes, the Messiah is here." Of course, you do not have to accept it if you do not want to. It is the free will of humanity to accept and accelerate the coming of the Kingdom, or reject and decelerate Its coming. There is no other way. That is the way to proclaim that we love the Lord.

***

Become a fisher of men. Let all know that you have found the Messiah, the Mehdi (Muhammad), the expected Buddha (**Maitreya**), the Christ (יהושוה), the Prince of Peace (Kumar = Prince), etc. Then we might unify All under One Banner of Salvation (**The Greatest Sign**). That is how you can serve **Maitreya** and become an instrument to spread this teaching.

As you spread the Word, you might find good soil to plant the seed of **Maitreya's** teachings. Then gradually each seed will grow into a mighty tree to give plenty of fruit, some thirty, some seventy, some a hundred…fold. This will lead to the fulfillment of **The Plan**. Those who have been prepared like you are just waiting for the call. They also will see answers to their questions, as you did, in **Maitreya** and His Teachings.

***

A lot of people hear about our teachings in this lifetime and are touched. Probably that was enough for them for the time being. The next lifetime they come back, they are cleansed in the period when they have not been on earth. When they come back they have already been touched by the Message, and they will come and become the champions of the cause and the Message.

But for us, those who really want to do the Will of God now, we have to be more discerning, more able to look at things and evaluate them. We cannot just accept anything offered to us, but we must clearly look at it and say, "Is this really a part of God's Plan, is it really His Will, is it a part of what He has demanded us to do? Or is this just my ego, or my tradition, or my own way that I want it to be done?" As more and more we accept what He said, we will see the benefit of it.

***

So, as Esa said, do not be worried about what you say. When the time comes my Father will put the words in your mouth, and you will say things that you know it is not you who is saying them. It is the Father. That is how the Spirit of the Father works right now with us, with the **Mission**.

When missionaries go out and open their mouths, the purer channels they become, the more submissive they are to the Message, and the more they let their egos go, the greater the works they will manifest, and the greater the Truth from the Father will come through them. That is going to have a greater effect on others because they will see that the Father is coming through them. That is how that flame is going to kindle a lot of other candles. And each candle lit can kindle many others.

So we really need the people who have been kindled first. If there is no kindling, there is no fire. No matter how good or beautiful our teaching is, or how many prophecies we tell them are fulfilled, the only thing they are going to say is "Why him?"

You tell them, "But who then?"

***

www.ingramcontent.com/pod-product-compliance
Lightning Source LLC
Chambersburg PA
CBHW081347040426
42450CB00015B/3335

what people are saying...

"Dear Voyagers: Join with us now as we travel to Planet Corrigan, a rare world where we discover the amazing, comical, and bizarre creatures which populate and animate an incredible atmosphere richly laden with a full measure of his prolific imagination. Gaze upon these works, ye mighty, and despair! These creatures live on multiple levels, and he who first enjoys them and then takes the time to contemplate their meaning will discover that beyond their hilarious first impression lurks a world of symbolism and deeper meaning. Laugh heartily, and take them to heart! You will not be disappointed."

—David B. Lee, Executive Vice President and Publisher, Remedy Health Media & former Senior Vice President, Magazine Publishers Association

"Take a trip inside the mind of Dennis Corrigan and you will be greeted with the Winged Jackass and the Weird Walkin' Stalker and much more. With "True Love Knows No Boundaries" Corrigan humorously takes no prisoners, and finally joins the ranks of Saul Steinberg, Charles Addams and Gahan Wilson."

—Steven Brower, author, designer and educator.

"The path described by genius is rarely straight or predictable. Such is eminently the case with the (*very*) peculiar genius of Dennis Corrigan. See if you don't find that to be the case as you leaf through this collection of characters (if I may call them that)—similar, from one to the next, only in their eye-popping, head-shaking, side-splitting, magnificent zaniness."

—James Manns: Ph.D., Boston University
Professor Emeritus of Philosophy, University of Kentucky
Author: Aesthetics (M.E. Sharpe, 1997); Reid and His French Disciples (Brill, 1994).

"The parallel universe inhabited by Mr. Corrigan and "friends" is both frightening and hilarious."

—Alice Drueding, Professor Tyler School of Art, Temple University

"I would like to spend five minutes in Mr. Corrigan's head ... but not a minute more."

—Joe Scorsone, Professor, Tyler School of Art, Temple University

"We can all be thankful that Dennis Corrigan decided to use his powers for good; I shudder to think what might have happened if he hadn't. Having breathed that sigh of relief, I can feel free to state the obvious: Corrigan is a genius. And this book proves it."

—Gerald Kolpan, journalist and author